NIGHT LIGHTS

To Arthur Sherman —
please enjoy!
Yours in poetry,
Jane Augustine

19. X . 05

NIGHT LIGHTS

POEMS BY

Jane Augustine

Jane Augustine

MARSH HAWK PRESS / 2004

FIRST EDITION

03 04 05 7 6 5 4 3 2 1

Marsh Hawk Press books are published by Poetry Mailing List, Inc., a not-for-profit corporation under United States Internal Revenue Code.

Grateful acknowledgment is made to the editors and the following publications in which these poems, sometimes under slightly differing titles, have appeared:

Hamilton Stone Review #2 (Spring 2004): "Reunion" and "Five Moons"
http://www.hamiltonstone.org
HOW2, v.1, #8 forum, "Memoire/Anti-Memoire" (Fall 2002): "History"
http://www.departments.bucknell.edu/stadler_center/how2
PoetsUSA "Focus on 9/11" (Fall & Winter 2002-2003): "Memoranda: September 15, 2001" http://www.poetsusa.com
Sugar Mule #1 (Fall-Winter 1995-1996): "Two Plans for Soho Street Performances," "Toronto in Winter," "A Folk Singer in Penn Station"
Water Voyages 9 (2002) in chapbook series with maritime collages by John Digby: "At the Mouth of Three Mile Harbor"

Many thanks as well to the editors of Marsh Hawk Press and Michael Heller for enduring support and friendship

Cover painting: from "Moonrise" by Jane Augustine
Book design: Claudia Carlson
Author photo: Michael Heller

Printed in the United States by McNaughton & Gunn

Library of Congress Cataloging-in-Publication Data

Augustine, Jane.
Night lights : poems / by Jane Augustine.
p. cm.
ISBN 0-9724785-9-0
I. Title.
PS3551.U388N54 2004
811'.54–dc22

2004013209

MARSH HAWK PRESS
P.O. Box 206
East Rockaway, NY 11518
www.marshhawkpress.org

For Ellen Ann Morley
and
her extended family

in memory of the ancestors

I am what is around me.
     —WALLACE STEVENS, "Theory"

At some point you realize
that it is not you looking at the moon
but the moon looking at you.
     —CHÖGYAM TRUNGPA RINPOCHE

Contents

PROLOGUE   IN SILENCE

Walking by flashlight
because the path is dark

the moon rising past rocks
spills white

over marshy gravel, showing
where to step away

from mud. No mud there.
No cloud here—

the willows quieted that
twittered with a pair

of yellow warblers earlier,
unseen water

running somewhere—
this tent farther

from a few voices,
nearer the moon's stripe

across the hilly meadow.

PART I   SHORELINES

Night

off Madeira, ocean and sky
indistinguishable

No night comes the same
        as any other, though similar. Change
           is its signal, as in the sough
     of waves that slap against rocks
              broken below cliffs. Night seems
             timeless with stars in place
        at first look, yet slowly passing
   to another station, if late,
later, sleepless, one looks again,
      and the sound, ceaseless, then
          is also not the same
      but subtly shifts its music
            within a range and sometimes
    bursts more loudly, strident
       almost, if wind upsurges.
                Night
   is steady, constant, at
a standstill in thought. Ocean
   and sky hold seamless,
          untampered with   until slowly
       at some point
          the immutable blue-black lessens
   and time starts up. It moves noisily.
        Night shrinks,
              disintegrates
       and those things have to happen, whether
one sleeps or seeks freedom, or denies,
     or wishes—after all—
        not to look at shadows.

Transformations

(i)

early morning, Madeira,
from the seaside hotel balcony

The long cirrus-shelf spreads across the world-width,
grows inflamed from the firepoint of the sun surfacing
just above the dark water-girdle rolling straight from
farthest left to farthest right, the eye-line now all crimson
blazing *red skies at morning*, enrouges the pink façades
of hotel towers sunk in pines where mossy verdure vests
umber-brown cliffsides in rubeate amberesque aura
intensifying green leafage and the hotel pools' aquamarine
through gold filters, and the sun's copper disc gradually edges
up under low scumble of grayish opaque cloud, white-streaked
and soft steely, as a luminous ray, a girder, goes aslant
the blurred bundles of a barren island and its ghostly twin
while the flame dissolves into a wash of pale yellowish
vacancy between ocean and emptiness invisibly lit as the fire
sinks back as if sucked down into the earth's volcanic core
and the sky normalizes into its generous equality of fire and light.

(ii)

the evening elements in all directions

mist	pale
surrounds	clouds
full	streaming
moon	outward
white	into
foam	night
laps	silence
rocks	sky

(iii)

Wind is rising
    and so is the moon
        out of sight
    in a cloud whirl
        in blue-black
            overhead and
straight out two
    amber dots, a tanker
        at rest now not
    a ship but a
        penetration of
            darkness where wind
whips the unseen
    sky and waves into
        endless sound

Now, and Memory: Quai d'Orsay

walking in Paris after a concert

Romance of the guitar. No escape
even in sharpest winter cold on
the Quai d'Orsay.

A surrender to now beyond body,
material, hour as it goes on
within — and on out

not stopping but stopped as
over the Seine in the blue-
metal dusk shone

the great gold sonorous moon.

*

Steel-gray clouds to the west still hold
a little light while the moon
full in the east

repeats itself in small gold moons
on the drive beside the river.
Bitterer wind

on the old, old stone bridge harries
the footsteps of the long dead,
the soon dying,

the composer gone to music,
the player gone with it into
the ripple of lights

on the mutable *bleu marine* Seine.

By the Rockwall on the Boat Channel

East Hampton: thinking of
Michelle Vu dying young

Orange gold wash
of sky above the lost sun:

blue darkness
rises from jagged black
of bushes, rocks:

tall weed's skeleton
rattles in the sea wind

dark masts pass
quietly into the dark harbor

*

Never again this sunset.
What confidence

that one can leap up at dawn tomorrow
raise a white sail,

clip safely outwards
on the sparkling solid blue.

At the Mouth of Three Mile Harbor

past sunset, no wind—
a fisherman on the black rock jetty
Water and sky gray-blue.

A ruddy flush on the horizon
darkens the channel
where the beach slopes

sideways back into reeds
by the old fishing station and
six picnickers have lit

a small fire. They look across
into the inlet's wine-dark
cedar trees and shadows

on the other shore
which thicken, move and rise,
evolve into a ship

with three tall masts
and blood-rose lateen sails,
purple as the dusk.

It glides out of hiding.
The deep blue hull parts
the waveless waters

under quiet power.
It heels into the channel.
The picnickers wave, call.

A horn toots. A flag
ripples from the stern
as it passes the jetty.
The masts point upward.
The sails grow taut
where harbor, bay and sky

meet night.

Water

We can repay our debt to our parents,
but we can never repay our debt to water
— JAPANESE PROVERB

The canal at Islington
runs straight gray
between low concrete bulkheads.
Straight bike path
runs beside it until the lock,
not much used
It's scummy there —
cottonwood fluff, algae,
tiny green specks afloat, caught.
Rebel backwater.
They should open the barrier sometimes.

*

Verticals of modern apartment buildings
with chrome-edged curtained glass
border the concrete channel.
Two swans cruise the water-road.
Their necks curve white against gray,
black masks over their knowing eyes.

*

at the Tate Modern with a friend

From behind the nearly-invisible glass
walls of the museum, the level Thames
that created London draws its fundamental
line, defines the squares, rectangles
of brick, halftimbers, basalt, girdered
steel, St.Paul's dome rotund and
light-attracting, establishes the business
of living firmly upheld by the gray-green
movement in stasis of water — and

across it the silver arc of the Millenium
Bridge and over on the right, a crane
constructing a highrise lifts two bright
red poles up out of the half-built mass
into the air, and from it a cable hangs
ready to hoist effortlessly many tons.

"Water is healing, isn't it?" she said,
pensive, beside me.

*

Melancholy. Is it bodily?
The body is mostly water
but its form is not water.

Is melancholy
thought or water?

*

The canal widens in an arc
overgrown with weedy shrubs
and trailing grasses where
the water is roughed up as
a red-hulled motorskiff,
tour boat, turns back at
the lock and goes under
the curved bridge, sort of noisy,
and the bike path humps
toward exit stairs which
present a choice of whether
to go on beside the water,
which would be succumbing
to desire to follow the canals—
a map shows how—
all the way across London,
the whole city—
         and out into the countryside
of 19th-century English landscapes,
under soft windblown blue sky, just as
here this afternoon.

a concert March 13, 2004

Heartbreaking to listen
to Shostakovich's Chamber Symphony
            "against war and fascism"
                        — Stalin censored Shostakovich —
            and to think of the Madrid dead for whom they played
" in memory of the victims"
                        this music, the long
                        trickle of water on a single violin.
A trickle   but ascending drop by drop
            against gravity, against the weight
            of destruction
                        — buildings, bodies, millions,
            many millions of Coventry, Dresden
Stalingrad, Hiroshima, an escalating
            scale of destruction.
                        Against it a few violins,
a relaxed unhurried wrist
            and a bow necessary
                        for sustenance —

but violas crowd in, and cellos
            agitated, furious —
                        this inner shriek
                                    of — you can't say
what neural thread grates under
            the gut-strung bows pushed to extremes

Music is like water,
            flows, swarms over obstacles,
formless, makes the form that holds it.

*

            on the train to Durham

Rainburst after sunny clouds.
More sudden sun dries
train windows, rainbow

vanishes. Low thunderous clouds
eastward vanish. White thunderheads
bulge south over "England's
green and pleasant land" —
the uncertainty of water.
Water overhead and wind
stronger. Less light. Gales
and rain. Will an umbrella
be needed, or will it change again
before the train reaches the station?

*

Tyneside, Newcastle,
coming and going

The train slows over the Tyne.
Noon light stipples the river,
opens its fan wide, wider
until the vestibule fills
with light, light, light.
Light blindedness:
no water nor bridge nor glass,
no eyes. Inundation detonates.

By night slow tide of the Tyne
slides for one moment
a blue crescent across the window,
not blue then but lighter black, a lost
ribbons of black, here and here and here,
a larger darkening:
no land nor water nor roads. A few amber holes
in unlit space, fewer, then none.

*

Proverbs of water
1) Water enlightens. Water and earth enlighten.
2) Water is not sunlight; earth is not darkness.
3) The sun of knowing resists the moon of unknowing.
4) Day for night to film, water to spread nightlights.

5) Rainy by day; misty at evening; invisible sleeping.
6) The lion drinks water, therefore water is stronger than he.
7) Beware the oxymoron of "holy water".

*

Commentary on rainwater: an echo

Not a thing
depends
upon a thick
black
stick glazed with
clear
nailpolish beside
the bleached
pulpit

Much depends
on seeing
rainwater

*

Too conceptual this notion
of water as the feminine,
the unconscious, shapeless.
She is the vessel, not what
is poured into it

*

Psychoanalysis of water: keep looking.
Don't read too much into it.

*

Literarily, water is limpid,
crystalline, a mirror, long fingers
touched to a damp forehead.
Forget that. Literally, it is—
        well, how can you say
        what anything is?
        "Is" is not

*

ah
ah
ah
falling water—
how water must fall
hidden waterfall
as it pours through the body.
The mountain stream flows
over and around rock and crags—
how it must fall away

*

The Danube flows lazy
broad and gray-green between
the castle on Buda hill
and parliament on the shore
at Pest, joining
and separating.

Water is wise.

*

Music—Bach, Brandenburg
in the ornate green and gilded hall,

thus a mind only of music
and then the full moon over the towers

of Budapest. Gold floodlights embellish
the classic columns of the museum

and against the night sky light up
a winter tree's twined branches

in golden curves of Secession art
hung with seedpods concealing

some kernel of fruit to come, consonant
with the moon and the gold,

an opening up to which the mind,
like the river, constantly moves.

*

Hard water.
Mineral rich and a problem,
as, for instance, the need
to clean it out of the plastic cup
in my daughter's bathroom
in Paris, the one the boys use.
Hard-water scale has built up
inside the cup's bottom
and grease on the top and
outside where fingers grab it.
Not noticeable. An absurd
obsession to scrub and dig
to scratch the scale away
and peel back the scum with
the round end of a nailfile,
the only tool at hand. Not
worth the effort, of course,
but I think it makes the water
taste a little better.

*

looking at "Montagnes célestes,"
Chinese paintings at the Grand Palais

The mountains and waterfalls,
peaks among mists, are spiritual

though also fine-ground black ink — earth —
and shaded grays out of a wetter brush.

Bone-stroke makes a branch broken,
nail-stroke the sharp pine needle

against the white brume rising
from the abyss, the unseen depths

But the white isn't water but paper
left blank, an emptiness, radical freedom.

The mountain is still there, a thousand
jagged edges, half-peaks, cliffsides

hiding the path on which the tiny figure
at the bottom sets a hermit's foot.

PART II   MOUNTAINS

Five Moons

over the Wet Mountain valley, Colorado,
in the driest summer known

(i)

Crescent growing   also falls in slow arc
    into darkness rising   behind pines:
        dish of pearl dips
    into marine blue black

(ii)

Half a lemon ripens   at tree height,
    its juicy gold geometry above
        a ruddy sunset:
    wishful grace of drink

(iii)

Gibbous   hefts itself   swings icy high,
    effaces stars on the stilled
        black curtain: straw-dry meadow
    looks midnight snowy

(iv)

Bronze copper, huge, round   dwarfs the far hills.
    Soft gong throbs silent light.   Cloud
        lowers iron shutters,
    jagged edge of knife and omen

(v)

Now just this: the earth not in the sun's way.
    A perfect ivory mirror reflects the eye
        opening.   Simply full moon,
    pine trees, dusk on the road-curve down

Jazz Festival

in the Sangré de Cristo mountains

without much beginning—a few bass
notes, a tryout, slips into the main
theme, come sax, comes drums, now
a latin riff, maracas knock, shift,
brass ocean surf surge on cymbals, while
the sax runs and seeks—something—going
on in fun, a hurry, trips over its own
notes, snare snapsnapsnapBANG irregular

gold aqua tentroof stripes over
walmart chairs, yellow white grid,
a white green back, red tee-shirt shoulders
—festival tee-shirt—Monk tune, Miles,
Sangrés bluish in the distance, clouds
gathering for maybe rain   woman reads
supine on an army blanket amid the chair army,
young midriffed suntans on the grass

GNU BLOOZE loud through the sax jounces
pinkhaired hand on a near knee   sky graying
brings far mountain into keener focus,
olive green slides Horn Peak into Comanche
Basin, high dark bluegray pines spread
up to treeline, not surely defined at any
particular altitude but then ending
in stony scree   and bass whomps like water

pours when we hear the persistent creek
among the alpine fir straggle on Goodwin
lake edge but nothing like saxophone,
that blatant man-metallic voice wobbles
into its non-ending, a human handful, so
many hands clapping is one footclomp or

what sound? Break   Clifford Jordan:
Blue Monk's stronger brass and gut job

lets go as the southmoving cloudbank
blurs the high not so far peaks into a flat
steelblue gray line against lighter gray so
 mountains appear and disappear inseparable
from form and color.   And art, isn't it
the quintessence of interpretation too,
the melody line like an unstateable divagation
from nothing previously known, hence

no divagation nor anything divagated from,
and a final mellowing out and sun
from somewhere.   *In Walked Bud* more
Monk Theloniously to raise the question
of again piano inseparable from its note
and elusive as mountains covered by
vapor, fog, something evolving out of
nothing   or am I always making a mistake

thinking of what to do next while
piano notes unfold precise as aspen leaves
when random sun hits?   no one body
in this audience is like any other nor
blade of grass under any picnic cooler
nor has any horn ever blown out quite
that exact reverberation   a deaf boy
signs to someone near the end

of a chair row. What comes through
his hearing-aid is just about all we hear.
Three young guys out on the lawn who
played before and maybe-teen girl in black
shirt, buttocked in denim cutoffs—no
way to record each one solo who
will disappear yet leave a past
behind   Piano endless in takeover

like mountain, like water, a
reclamation. Lightning leaps over
Spread Eagle Peak. Thunder *'Round
About Midnight* as the broody afternoon
gives warning to my arms with its
lengthening chill. Not even music
guarantees continuance. Blues seventh hovers—
pauses—improv, stops.   That's it.   Face it.

At the Summer Solstice

Last night my father's deathnight
twenty years ago
who was born

the eve of the solstice,
the longest day.
Tonight overhead

the sun gone, the stars
in their far niches
bright as if

for us, for me. What to say
of their truth,
his truth?

On the cabin's unlit deck
the protective railing
about to give way,

star-molecules bind with
swimming cells in
this body, named

and futile in decline, also
perhaps with stray
cancer cells there—

like his—or here.
The darkening light
reveals sky

as it is, mostly empty,
yet seeming full

of tiny fires,

burning worlds so distant
they relieve a mind
unthinking it will go,

will go.

Night Lights

above Westcliffe, Colorado

Ranch yard lights in the valley—
scattered, not many.

Isolate. One drop of water,
one musical note, one thought
where the black lake overruns.

*

Deep blue early night
held the crescent moon.

Clean light, a high curved
window opened a slot
until a dark peak closed it.

*

It's more quiet
than I've heard it.

The color of ink.
Not a cross hatch, not blank.
The basis.

*

Nightfall under steely clouds.
Amber arclights ten miles away
at the ballpark in town.

      Are they playing?
      Always.
It is the play of the mind.

Behind, through a window,
a crescent moon, misty.
      Is the glass unwashed?
      It can't stay unspattered.

*

Six starry floodlights
have come on over the ballpark.
      "Without thought"
      the crowd watches.
The creek whispers ease
downstream in that direction.

*

You know those lamps
with motion sensors
that protect doorways?

Pain comes on suddenly
that way, a hot blossom
too white on the sidewalk.

You don't know where
the invisible line is
that set it off.

Someone else must have placed it.

*

I drove south of town alone
in the entire blue-black night
without end. The half moon darkened it.

     Gone valley, gone road
     past the headlights' shallow pool
     into desert.

Roadless road deep into the Huerfano,
"orphan" country.

Twenty years ago the radio played
Bye Bye Miss American Pie.

*

The guitar plays
     recuerdos, memories.
         Midnight condenses

chilled mountain air
     on the old deckrail
          that leans outward.

Unsafe. It is breaking.
     Feel it—the splinters.
          Silver notes. Needles

in the eyes,
     the million-eyed
          River of Heaven.

*

Holding the little boy
the night before they left,
meteors streaked the sky.

     The thought returns as the Perseids,
     wisps of light. A gap.
          —*I have driven a road*

by starlight alone. And will again
   It's hopeless,
          this lack of fear, this fear.

     Someone leans heavily on the rail.
     It creaks. The very distant
     lights of town squat unblinking

but the massed black pines
intervene.
          "Oh look, it
lasted long—"

          More quiet.

The far high night is breathing.

Permeable Membrane

(i)

Note on the telephone pad
beside the seven digits: *n.a.*
no answer

but music from radio to ear
permeates, answering
no word.

The bell rings at the Great Gate
of Kiev, a picture
exhibited.

Where is here? The skin,
that fascinating organ
of the body,

manufactures its useful raincoat
to keep one thinking
of an other.

(ii)

Another—it is all "other."
Outside, the blue sky overswept
by clouds registers
     as if eyes
         saw something. A mind
      reads the alpine firs among
      scrub oak and thinks "time"—

To know they are there
growing. The words don't do it.
You don't have
     the right idea.

                The bluejay caws
what word? No idea
        fits the knowing. Natural
and unnatural align
in *no answer.*

The radio's off but not
the ear. Beethoven deaf—

        how did he do it?

                        (iii)

So this imagined self within manufactures
as protection its imagined skin

while the imagined other—but not
so imagined, or one couldn't open an eye.

It's a crazy business, those who see
UFOs, hear voices, hear the stories

they want to hear, as if manufacturing
their own dollar bills.
                        But a bird's

sharp note sounds outside and
it is not distorted mind that rides it

into the pines whose needles fall always
and whose brown-black branches crawl

with a golden parasitic flower that kills
the tree, eventually, in which now sits

the warbler, *empidonax.* Scientists
have named it in a book, and so its breast,

faintly streaked yellow, and its wild flycatching
are truthful, though hardly a guide, not music.

Divided Creek

meditating on nations in a wet season
when the creeks run high

Creek divided
by willows and boulders,
the white water plunges

under the hikers' bridge.

*

Rebel whinny
of a horse
somewhere in the campground
where they stake them
before the rodeo.

Has one escaped?
Where can he go?

*

Division "of opinion"
over Iraq, Israel, Palestine.
Past midnight
a long resounding shot.

*

The quiet night is one night,
moon in the sky all morning.

*

When I walked
under city streetlights
through leaf-shadows,
my feet grew shadows.

Enlightened, endarkened

I was walking
on hard trails.

*

No more whinny.

Did they catch him?
Where did they take him?

Would you think the absence
of headlines a trustworthy sign?

*

Long division
of breakage and dissolution
one may not speak the word for—

say "prison" or "patriot"

say "Rosita cemetery"

*

So, my friend, the cop ticketed you
for a moving violation.

Were you just pissed off
at the slow-moving asshole
on the freeway?

Do you think you're justified—
it's the other guy's fault?

You don't think
this has anything to do with
Israel vs. Palestine, do you?

Or Serb vs.Croat
or Taliban, the way it's
starting up again—

*

Under the bridge
the creek comes together.

Its clear pools
hold a sky-fragment.

Then it splits again six ways
under the thickening willows.

*

The mountains are high
hideouts.
They keep clear water
falling.
You can peel and eat
the inner bark of willow
if you are starving.

That shot—
who fired it?

Did it miss?
Where is the gunman?

The Hikers

internal monologues, below thought

Father

Middle age pulls mother
after, pushes son ahead.
Not to push. Try to do it
the way we did, I
age 9, going somewhere

Older son

BOR-ing! So slow. No
thing goes so   slooooooow

Feet   heat   knap-
sack just   going. Bugs.

Bugged   BORed. What
is this nothing
happening for?

Younger son

Bounce. Run, run
back to my brother.
I get to carry
the canteen. (bounce)
I keep up with my
brother and my father.
Go, go, with my brother
who carries the fishing pole.
Trail up. Slow. Trees.
My brother goes around
the big tree curve.
Hurry up so I can still
see him

Oma

Fireweed, bed-straw, hare-
bell, Indian paintbrush,
kinnikinnick—also called Indian tobacco,
bearberry—showy daisies
orange and black butterfly: fritillary
white butterfly: cabbage

yellow? another kind of cabbage?
It chooses to land on yellow flowers.

So much unnamed

Mother

We and the woods are one.
The boys, big and little,
green growth. It is slow,
cool, sunny—a relief.
They are far along the trail
and I walk at leisure
left alone, finally,
in the silence of
sweet-smelling pines

Philosopher, trailing behind

Who writes the poem
when the waterfalls
plunge over boulders?

The reflected aspens
twitch on the pond's surface.
A green thicket of willows

over swamp muck.
Nature is too unformed.
I want a hand in it,

my pen on the mottled page.

Rocks and Water

(i)

Water falls over
rocks. Rocks hold water. Fallen
trees hold moss above

and in water. A bridge
crosses rocks under falling
water. Little boys climb

between beams holding
the bridge. They sit on rocks
beneath the wooden

planks. They look around.
One fishes in a deep pool.
One carries a peeled

aspen stick. One says he wants
to do things "tout seul,"
climbs away

from constant waterflow.
The others' voices not
audible among

water-sounds and tumult
of falling, staying,
growing. Not solid,

neither rock nor water.

(ii)

The trees are tall, their trunks
bare until the top. The tallest
trees lie fallen.

The stream cuts a deep gorge
out of which the trees rise,
their green tips

lashed by wind that brings down
alpine fir and aspen both.
The wind and sky

invisibly hold each branch
or strip it. Each leaf
or needle separately

falls into the painting
in the mind's eye. The boys crouch
happily under

the bridge which shades them. The
shade passes. The sun heats
the rock. Flies alight

because they like sweat and skin,
ephemera that die in a day
on the great slab of stone

embedded beside the bridge.

PART III   LAKE PARADOX

Fireside

at Lake Paradox in the Adirondacks

The cricket's flutes, tonight
are broken....

Oh I am alone!
Who knows my tonight's feeling!

—YONE NOGUCHI,
THE SUMMER CLOUD, 1906

What can be said to a woman
whose daughter has set fire to herself?

The night is cold.
She lit a fire in the parlor
after she phoned the hospital
        in Tennessee.

Packed in ice, unconscious,
        will live, probably.

Silence before the unstable flames.

*

Alone, the fire burns.
Give it another long-burning log.

*

Here is an old book with misprints
mistranslated in skin-grafted language.

Awareness is said to be
"the fire that consumes the fuel
of conceptual mind."

Is awareness madness?
Oak wood there
fanned by updraft
glows neon.

*

Questionable, the death wish.
The incandescent log hums, a holdout.

*

She gazes into the fireplace
    I am alone ...

Rust-orange leaves,
an armful, curl and dry
in a smoky vase on
the parlor sidetable.

A red taillight's comet
zips past the window.
        Who knows my ...

*

Science of flame, of burns,
how to promote healing—

this is written in a magazine.
She reads it, I read it.

A log breaks, drops
behind the fire-screen.

*

"Let die what must die"
means "don't let die
what must not."

Third-degree thoughts eat
past the outer layers.

The burned one's temperature
falls. Nurses heat the hospital room.

*

It's not enough — "non-thought."
Living is thinking, hardwood.

*

... tonight's feeling?

Tonight doesn't exhibit
personal emotion. It is

simply tonight.

A trace.
A line of ink.

*

The solar fireball isn't
always there, luckily,
to cause its mayhem.

Science of doing good for others..
Find that book and read it
      by its own light.

Moongazer

in an Adirondack camp

The ivory moon moves silently beyond the
      drooping black lace of the cedars.
The dark air holds the cedars' lightly acrid
      odor in silence.
How lovely is the moonlight—how soundlessly
      the old song sings
I walk a-down the meadow with no one
      near me—
Invisible the deep damp grasses beyond black
      shrubbery's soundlessness.
A slant of light falls onto the screen porch,
      a faintly off-white blur.
The darkness darkens coming up through the cedars,
      a palpable presence
amid the forest shadows—feel it, the pressure
      of the changing night and the moon
not quite full, a potential, but in brightness
      already enough, *how lovely*—

No Moon

Overcast sky, moon hidden. It seems
that lights indoors must be sufficient.
The sun-aged brown of the high livingroom's
unfinished walls makes the lamplight gold
on the upright piano, the desk, end-tables.
The lamps on bases of bronze or saffron glass
stand as if flambeaux in a medieval hall or
sconces in gimbels in a ship's hold, enough
to see the thick timbers and crossbeams
and support-posts that reach into dim heights
above the window's many opaque panes,
where, last night, the moon took precedence
in chill simplicity. Tonight is less sublime:
rugs underfoot, books on the sofa, heaters
turned up, and ordinary conversation.
A newspaper rustles, a page turns: inner life
as if the piano's ivories played themselves.

Rainy Night Thoughts

Green, green, I want you green
— LORCA

It rained all day.
Rain is green,
Greeny masses—trees
leafy bushes—grew greener
as rain drenched them
and the grass swam
in greening pools beyond
the porch screens.
Rain is sky outside
glass and cloud
over gray glass lake just past
dark gray pines dripping
silver, and an inside
sursurrus on the tin roof,
the whir of the green
engine and constancy
of water. It is raining
all night. Sleepless
rain thrums its thoughts
hard on the roof, irregular
overabundant green,
green light within.

Meaning the Random

Sometimes it's too much effort
to search for meaning.

Why search? It'll still be there.
We talked at the dinner table.

The pool of light over the pansies,
yellow in the small vase, means as much

as the silent girl to whom we
never thought to put questions

to draw her into the conversation
on Bulgaria and a bank card

stuck in a Barclay's ATM—or
the night before, at another

dinnertable, lace-covered,
fine Wedgewood almost oriental

in design, held the flan, and the nice
white-haired Olsons, midwest born,

chatted with pleasure at being
here visiting their cousin Sara—

they were doing a puzzle in
the livingroom, a 500-piece

jigsaw, and we each after much
searching found one piece to fit in.

Today, a Victorian Painting

at Lake Paradox

Through sliding glass doors, clarity:
Frost still glitters on the deck outside.
Slice of hot sun on the scarred table top.

Gold knotty-pine walls and low-beamed
pine ceiling grow a tamed wilderness
around the high old oak chairs.

Corner tea-cart carries green cacti. Its
overflowing red blossoms fall to a faded
blue mud-rug where sprawls a brindle cat,

white belly upturned in warm white light.
A woman sits reading in a red shirt
and dark fleece vest, a red knot

at the end of her braid. The wall clock
stopped at 2:45 early in the last century.
Its intricate brass-flowered pendulum

catches the modern moment's all-
pervading shine and heat of each
lustrous object as, out there, vast sky

widens beyond the apple tree's
clinging leaves and snow-trace
among weeds down the riverbank.

Brilliance shapes the table's rim,
the reader, the book's glossy pages, a knife
silver on a glass plate, and a biscuit

half eaten. The salt cellar's chrome
turret blinks a tiny beacon under the deep
fern-green fronds out of which rises

a flower-mountain of mauve heather
and lilac phlox among wine-red
freesias opening their tawny star-centers

in a swath around six perfect roses whose
just unfolded petals, apricot-peach-orange,
hold onto the morning light and make it last.

PART IV   ARTS

A Suite For and From Paula Rego

I. The Painter Depicts Her Mother's Death

a diptych

(i)

The plump white baby holds
her doll mother straddled on her knee.

The pompadoured mother pouts
lipsticky lips at the baby's inert mouth.

Not a baby but a ponytailed child.
Now one sees the mother less small

in blue business suit and high heels.
The baby-child clutches her doll to her,

strong left hand pulling up the blue
skirt. The mother kisses goodnight

the tearful girl-child in the chair marked
with crosses of blood on the slipcover.

The blood comes from their spread legs,
the monthly ending, a streak of red

where the mother presses against
the daughter's baby-fat belly.

The eyes of both are shut.
The time for seeing passed unseen.

(ii)

The strong black-browed woman lifts
the mother's porcine body, a meat package

in loose paper, as a teenager might
carry her pet German shepherd.

Her arms are lost in the burden's
black folds. Terrified mother's face
looks away, mouth wide in outcry.
Daughter's eyes, ink smudges, sink back

into the need. Ink-stroke mouth
neither droops nor smiles. It sets

the raised foot's direction. The woman
wears sensible shoes, black loafers,

and a freemoving plaid skirt with red
crosses in its folds. Water dropped

on the paper and made a cloud
over the mother's distraught white hair.

Green underfoot—is it grass or
floor, as under the baby's armchair?

The daughter carries the mother forward.
The daughter's sleeve is blue, not quite

the blue of the mother-doll's dress.
The woman's cheek has the faintest pink

of warm blood circulating under the cold
white paper that sharply holds the pen's edges.

II. Looking at a Woman's Paintings in Time of War

Yale Center for British Art

(i)

The gallery's high, cooled white rooms
with discreetly placed track lighting

opened space before the framed terror

of women alone but exposed, seen
where no one should be looking, as
a policeman's flash bulb has to record

brutalities, the mangled corpse, fatal
accidents—so the woman looks up
into her own camera as she squats

over a tin bucket, self-aborting.
She wears a common cotton print dress
and clunky high heels while she's bent

doubled over in pain for the terrible
impossible choice of holding on
to her own life at the cost, she knows,

of another's—impossible not to have
that knowledge placed permanently
in the accurate black strokes of the

lithograph. Don't underestimate
her necessities, says the painting.
Know she will bear the unbearable.

*

That day the television did its concealing act
on a bombing. Many dead, but it ran
the same loop of "reality"—one wounded man
on a stretcher wheeled again and again
into an ambulance. No way to see
blown-up bodies, the maimed, the walls
fallen, or what is crushed under them,
or to look into the eyes of the grief
of the mother who wants—wants—
what can be known of her wants
once the cameraman leaves?

Another woman cowers
in a wingchair, knees to chest,
feet pulled up off

the terrifying floor
away from the stout, unconscious
—dead?—old female body

flopped out supine
beside the chair, too close,
front and center

in a cheap shiny slip,
lace-trimmed, those legs
spread, thick and white.

In the mirror, the chair's
back corner and the woman's
crooked elbow, yellow sleeve,

and a child—a girl who holds
a large mask, crude with eye-holes,
in her arms like a doll.

The viewer, beyond the frame,
becomes the child who looks
with minor fascination

on the nearby lust and horror.
On the far left, a thin black
supervisory matron in profile

benignly gazes downward,
walled off in another room. She is
that other viewer who does not see.

The body on the floor
does not appear in the mirror.
When will the girl put on the mask?

So far she hasn't.

III. The Painter Does Little Red Riding Hood

a five-panel installation

(i)

In the old tale the mother is missing almost altogether. Anyway, she's no help. She has only useless advice to offer the daughter who's going into the deep woods of sexuality. "Ta-ta," she said, "now don't go off the path," meaning stick to the virgin path of bourgeois marriage leading to the sexless safety of old age — "Grandmother's house."

Now, in the new tale, the mother is very much present, protective. She knows the dangers as she embraces the daughter, both in their deep blood-red sexually luxuriant dresses. The mother's ladylike high-heeled left foot is placed between the girl's feet, blocking the way to what lies between her legs but also balancing and supporting her. The distant grandmother, half man half woman in his/her running shoes and red boxing shorts, head draped with a peasant's babushka, looks on, a bit out of it, androgynous, not clear in the child's mind.

(ii)

But the daughter is on the edge of adulthood, edgy, trying to escape from childhood. See those sharp blood-red lacquered nails. She's ready. She's gotten her period. She knows there's something highly interesting outside the window she's poised to climb out of. Sneaky and not quite innocent, though appealing with her plain little girl's mug, looking back to see if anyone's watching.

(iii)

The wolf—well, yes, like Coyote the trickster, the shape-shifter, he looks just like a man, except you know he's not a man because he doesn't wear shoes. He's a meat eater, found on every . streetcorner and in Mike Leigh movies. He's scruffy, unwashed, arrogantly showing off the tattoo and the hairy chest, a little too old, but the young girl's eyes can't see that. Naturally he chats her up. When she takes off her red riding-hood, you see she's wearing a green dress. She's very green, inexperienced, but doubtful, wondering why her grandmother has a beard and moustache. Children find old women most odd, smelly, misshapen, speaking foreign words, Another species of being, possibly from another planet. The peculiar eyes, big ears, big teeth. But she doesn't have time to know she's made a mistake in playing the game of this guy purporting to be trustworthy. He just eats her.

(iv)

The child disappears from the paintings, and the mother re-appears in her red dress. Is this the good mother, who's usually dead in fairy tales, come back to life? Not quite. The child is gone. She has become her own mother reincarnate out of the blood of her broken hymen to take revenge. With her satanic pitchfork, she's going to rip open the dead beast bloated with misused power that killed him. She's freeing herself from everything that swallows up women. No doubt she'll pitch the damned deceiver into a Dantean bolgia.

(v)

She takes what's useful that is left of him, his pelt of self-assurance. She adorns herself with silver-tipped furs, the wolf's inert black head conspicuously caught under her arm. She's quite smart in her scarlet ensemble and her red-winged hat, looking off to her left just as the girl did earlier but with more knowing skepticism. Is it a job interview? Anyway, she's qualified. Experience has not gotten the better of her; she's mastered it. No external rescuing woodsman needed here. No one can rescue you but yourself. One more phony myth of women's niceness and weakness bites the dust.

Two Plans for Soho Street Performances

— "Real Life: The Movie" (headline NY Times)

(i)

Put on a huge black mourning veil,
    waistlength all around, over
        an opaque skin-colored stocking
        facemask with 3 equal-sized 1"
        holes for 2 eyes and 1 mouth
        & 2 tiny 1/2" nostril openings

But the black veil will be thick so
        the inner face will hardly
        be visible

Wear a shabby loose print dress
        ripped black stockings & scuffed
        Girl Scout oxfords

Walk along the streets of Soho,
        invisible eyes downcast
        head bent forward

Carry a placard 8-1/2" x 11"
        lettered large black on white
        & pinned to the back of the dress

        under the veil but readable

SHADOW

Sit on selected doorsteps. Plan
point of entry, secluded & place
of departure. Time it.
            In a cracked black plastic handbag
      carry & play a tape of female dialog:

Q. What is your name?
      A. *My name is Lee Jun*
        Q. Are you a nun?
          A. *I am none, no nun*

Q. Are you doing art?
    A.   *No art*
        Q. Are you crazy?
            A. *No insane*
Q. Are you in mourning?
    A.   *No morning, no evening*
        Q: No?
        A: *None even*

Sit down on the sidewalk
next to a mailbox
or fire hydrant.

    .   .   .

    Think of a way to end this performance.

(ii)

Female figure in very high heels, very tight
    '50s suit with huge rhinestone dog collar
        (real dog collar from pet store) leans

on a cane. 8-1/2" x 11" sign on her back

CLOUD OF UNKNOWING

Head covered by white sheer stocking with
    holes for 2 eyes & mouth under a white
        cloud of bubble netting, made by

stripping paper off a big Japanese lampshade
    (round) so the thin metal arcs support
        the netting—
                but better:

a male figure (evidently) in very shiny shoes,
    tightwaisted Italian silk suit, necktie leans
        on what feminine object: broom?

Same head but
in an invisible cloud
with an unseeable sign.

    What is the drama to be performed?

The Protectors

Musée de Guimet, Paris

(i)

Light and glass expose and protect
the ancient terracotta figures
    twenty-five hundred years old.
Seated women, hair piled high, play
    musical instruments. A horse
arches its splendid neck and turns
    its sad eyes toward a stone groom.
It mourns its master, for whose tomb
    it was shaped. The fingers gone
to dust still live in the curved clay,
    more than mortal, less than
eternal, a reminder paused
    under fixed spotlights.

    Shakyamuni walked
from village to village in India,
reminding women and men that everything
    changes and makes us suffer.
    No lasting self then or now
in those sculptors, but there are the objects.
    A few notes of music
        pass the viewer's ear and vanish.

(ii)

The savage dark-blue Mahakala,
"protector of the teachings,"
reaches out from the thankha's canvas.
His eyes roll and flames surround
the flailing arms that knock away
one's ego, arrogance and fakery.

Could I have felt his power if I
hadn't dreamed her, a woman

in an aureole of fire blocking my path
up marble monumental steps
in New York City? Blue-black, intelligent,
ferocious mother-self, she turned me back—

to what? But she was with me.
And these are with me too, these
painted lotus-seated ones among
their red-orange jadegreen thoughts
row on row, luminous, who reach out
of an enormous floor-to-ceiling scroll
to chain the sun and take on death.

Draughtsmanship, or What is Not in the Portrait

an exhibit in the British Library

Albrecht Dürer with one hand drew the other finely,
at age thirteen himself in silverpoint, which can't be corrected.

The fine eye, the real tool, is only in the mirror.
The replica ruthlessly insists on being taken for reality.

The real hand is gone; the stroke it laid in copper stays.
Fine line next to finest builds to likeness recognized.

This my hand, veins bulging, makes its clumsy mark.
Proportion is truth: the eye is smaller than one supposes.

The ground blue-green or ivory set off inks now brown.
In charcoal shading a lighter gray defines the jaw's curve.

It is line next to line that assembles the semblance of faces.
Those eyes watch. What else but go on to another drawing?

For the Sculptor of Heads

*Marcelle Quinton, of whom it is said, truthfully,
she has "lived a blameless life"*

A blameless life
given to the sculpture of heads.
Here they are on shelves, evidence:
white oval marble on a plinth, black-glazed
on side tables and ranged
on the ascending cornice in the library.

The head holds everything, after all,
within its planetary globe.
The sculptor in her studio
strong-armed the earth into its proper shape,
the one skull that protects
the brain's entangled re-chargings.

She saw the head in its full truth
from all directions, witness
to the right seeing that leads to
making it right . No wonder
sculptors and conductors
of music live longest. The arm

swings wide and grows strong without
taint of aggression. Singleminded,
enjoying it, she hurls the clay
or chisels resistant marble until
the head takes form, and change
becomes permanent power.

On library shelves below the heads
the books arrayed contain the thoughts
that swarmed in those friable skulls
now bronze or stone, words in profusion,
other worlds. Thought without a thinker.
The heads are reminders, presences.

Live Painting

as in "live music," a word-paint experiment
with Lynn Umlauf in her studio

(i)

Live painting, or live paint:
you wouldn't say
        it is any thing.

        thing   think
        Ding an sich

the thick paper
(not made any more)
cut from a human-body-size
        sheet   had already a
        mark —*remark?*
on it for a start

        so no
violation of a pure
smoothness
        So we went on
        the painter first
fearless of course
bold black, porcelain turquoise,
        that Chinese stroke
                and the poet
                in terror
to make a mark.
        It isn't my thing—
                dared some chalk.
Cyclamen red came out
    of two hands.

Space makes
whatever is in it, though
that hasn't anything to do with it
either.
      Safe in danger,
       two figures at a table
        on which lie the dirty chalks,
inks, brushes

A circle of cadmium yellow
but not a complete circle
       the open end free,
           a lack of completion.

A worse danger.
      A whole hand palm
       spreads a brighter gold
          outburst
down
          and the phone rang
      so the one hand waited, held up
       covered with pollen
    because sometimes in respect
for the other's loneliness, one
        can't go on.

      One is afraid and goes on.
      One's not afraid and goes on.

      Lacquer nailpolish-red paint
swooped—couldn't bring myself
          to that, so the long
      circular black strokes
      at the side   wobbled

        Amateur, you see it
but it also didn't seem a black
          mark,

or three marks—
        "Don't put on more green,
    you're going too much to
    the center, you're spoiling it."
                Yes or no.
when to stop.   Just then,

        I thought walking home by Friends Seminary
under the leafy trees.

(iv)

He turned on the music. Suddenly
Beethoven's piano concerto #3.

It is about the two hands
and the ephemera of the permanent.

Not heard before just like this
but you recognize it,

not light or space but not
separate, either, from them,

but not an intrusion on the ear
which accepts the notes' wordings

that fingers have left behind.

(v)

Those Roman artisans who placed
the gilt mosaics into San Clemente's
vaulted heights over the crypt of Mithra
and peeling frescos of Constantine,
they were just working, like the ones
who first put the temple there
to light and darkness.
It was work in a high place
even then, over a subterranean river

that runs a long way,
is still running.
          Treble works in
with the bass, neither new nor old,
painting alive, live music, not
anything more than
ongoing.

PART V   CITIES

A Folk Singer in Penn Station

in memoriam, again,
for Michelle Vu

High pure notes of the girl's tremolo,
sad-eyed voice in last slow endings,
she sings where the escalator's slant chrome
bears upright bodies down onto marble
hard floors under TV schedule screens.
Cloud-moving winds of the faint guitar

and the birdsong sadness in a few faces
changes a little, mourning concealed in tall
black men—two in work jackets, not trees
swaying but they stand in breeze echoes,
in the swirling crowds pausing clustered
in gray raincoats, numb purses clutched,

brushed by an invisible falling dew
or halftears for whoever's lost, Irish
lad, or—oh my son to have had to lose her
to the slow earth far under the stone
floor, too slow and dark to come back
to green leaf music.   Here under mechanized

ad sign's ill glow, travelers oblivious to
journeys longer than a day flow high, higher
or sink, ignoring effortless clarity of air
and mountain stream spray flung out to vanish
past bird-call and evanescent lake silver
—my son, you listen to her lost voice

speaking on a tape, the lasting notes
replayed in lasting midnight darkness

in the long concourse this side of
the river of forgetfulness.
                              The screen shifts.
The train announced, the herd swarms down
other gray stairs where the great metallic worm
swallows and abolishes the water-notes descending.

Perspective

The jury room exudes utilitarianism. No one's utilizing it
so, under the general fluorescence, it becomes a painting..
Teal blue leatherette chairs with faux walnut arms set up
a greenish wave—several waves—across beige linoleum,
the next wave-series more blue, then darker blue. White
light lines a foamy edge to each plastic curve. Peach shirt
lumps on the right. Cobalt shirt against the walnut wall
punctuated by a tiny brass lock and hinges. Up front,
focal point, a shiny gold half-globe top of a waste can
raises its robot helmet head among the black curled
or coiffed spheres afloat over the ivory shirt, white shirt,
spread newspapers and half-open book in a high hand
poised above the waves. A nose in profile, mostly hidden,
contemplates the page held up to partially obscure
the rosebrown paneling, pale tan rack of magazines,
blue sign white-lettered NO SMOKING by the bright
brass-finialed red and white slant-slashed American flag.

Progression

Never a day without a line of poetry...
—HORACE

a meditation in shih *form*

(i)

Inbound on the Long Island Rail Road

Never a day without writing a line of poetry,
never a journey that ends with wheels' silence.
The body, sick, sits in the iron tunnel unmoving
as the firewheel vanishes and the icewheel rises
on the computer screen of space, specks of dust
emptying out. Overground the city's cryptic icons.
Underground the purring power muffles ego-sleep
of selves, shadows, lights passing the lethal track's repairs.

(ii)

East Side, 10 a.m.

November day without a line of poetry but plenty
of doctors, defiant walk for health in mind beside
the silver river and concrete hospital bunkers.
Warning lifts its smoke threads out of Con Ed's
ominous chimneys. Resistance of footsteps
on the walkway over blind traffic-roar. Little
pump under the breastbone, countermusic
relentless, recycles its inner Leonids' star-storm.

(iii)

Midday: street sounds

Wrench, pluck, extract a line of poetry—
from where?—to override loud dread of silence
in the radio-laden air. Pipe a new line to earphones
walking deaf under the medical center canopy.

They die in there, other selves, wired to glucose
and monitors. "…be late," a cellphone maunders.
Brakes shriek near thing, engines snarl forward,
away, away. A friend is dying, and it is soundless.

(iv)

Sundown: hospital view

The firewheel falls again behind highrise towers.
Window-eyes ignite in million watt surveillance,
mimic protection. Night softens the icewheel's edge
bent over the black river. What line of poetry for one
who, saved by surgery, weeps for his friend who wasn't,
for failed chemo, ticking I.V., whatever hides beyond
a door signed "oxygen in use," for himself a shadow
trailing the street-siren's long cry: pain, disaster.

(v)

On the outbound train

Stitched belly barely healed, the body sleeps
underground, now lit, now lost as the power breaks.
Track repairers pass in orange vests, armored signage.
Overground, the city empties behind. Instant
windows frame the Queens necropolis and lose it fast.
For the funeral attended, for the dying eye's swift blink,
for hopeless postponement, never a day without
a line, never a journey that ends in wheels' silence.

Toronto in Winter

(i)

At sunset

the sub-zero world outside
      the 35th-floor hotel window
            requires a pearl gray palette

for the lake's distances.
      Peach gray sky rises to
            palest overhead blue.

Glass walls' green gray
      embossed by gold loopholes
            darkens as steam heat plumes

upward past the highest spire.
      The rust brick blocks
            thicken below. Snow lies

thin on a roof-ledge sinking
      back into blue blur. The sun falls
            away off on the right

beyond the string of harbor lights.
      Tiny taxis, beady-eyed,
            travel tiny black-gray avenues

at the bottom of the perpendicular.
      It is deep gray inside the
            the pearly sheer drapes

that frame the multi-cubic vista
      as the spume unfurls higher into
            mauve efflorescence

and lights in other towers come on and on.

(ii)

With moonrise

from the 35th-floor hotel window
the darkness of skyscrapers
comes alive.

Cargo laden glass-sided
bulkheads almost move out
to sea.

The moon, a tossed ball,
faintly silvers the spire,
the mast

of the monumental city-ship
anchored in the freezing
blue black.

Boxes of light wrap bands
around the towers
between

bands of hollow box-caves
of unlit windows.
The great

buildings take their stone
out of mountains, glass out
of sand,

their size out of oceans
and physics. Under the moon
they enlarge

the sky. The towers
are bioluminescent. Light
always astounds.

Inside the 35th-floor window
the heated dark deludes and comforts.

The moon paints

a pale rhombus on the carpet,
as if one might forget the heights
or the intense cold.

For the Psychoanalyst on Her 70th

If you look across First Avenue
at the windows in brick highrises
—at least 70 windows in sight—

you could think of the 70th
as 70 windows you looked into
or 365 times 70 mornings of seeing

into minds and foibles, and they too
through their curtains looking back.
What a mix—the blue-eyed sky,

sunlight, the straight heights,
too stark and boxy for the lives
contained, a base out of which

they spill into what they're doing
to fix up the grounds—what a mess
of constant up-digging,

gray excavations, slime,
earth-movers, but surrounding
new green, like that—also daffodils,

tulips red leftover, a few, and
sudden Japanese-y pink puff-clouds
on wet black boughs, and dogwood

lurid and exuberant where two guys
winch some impossible weight up
a shrouded wall. The ropes

sway. Patiently they loft it there,
up over the top, whatever it is—
70 years like that—

Reunion

at a Quaker women's college

Classmates, we are a Society of Friends,
the true internet, non-electronic, kept together

by reunions, e-mailings, phoning and photos.
The past links to the present in a worldwide web.

These words are part of it. One thought-thread lightly
flung out catches another's and lightly connects.

A door opens. You look into a garden, seeing
butterfly-bush that bloomed in your own backyard,

although, as in Vermeer, the doorway with its slant
of sun is the point of most interest. This internet

of women's lives began for us many years ago
through mere proximity, by accident.

Making friends is not agenda-driven, like
marriage or love that insists something should happen.

Your friends at a distance watch the work going on
in you, mute. Unknowing they sense it. The thread holds.

Rilke said poets living together should pledge
to "respect each other's solitude," for the form

of a poem — or of the ultimate artwork,
a life — will only come out of formlessness when

given space. A canvas, for instance, depicting
windowed half-light that shines on a pregnant woman

holding a balance scale in her right hand. Not much
overtly is known about what's growing within,

but death and life hang in a balance unspoken—
not unsayable but too much—and thus the net's

gaps mean as much as its knots. The seventeenth-
century Quakers sat in meeting, silent, enjoined

from speaking till the great urge not to speak
had arisen, not to break silence frivolously.

But when the light within came to a woman,
she spoke, and no one forbade her. A world-change.

We are her heirs, heiresses, wealthy in speaking,
distributing the wealth. The network expands that raised

stone archways and let light through library windows,
that made our minds libraries, studios, gardens.

It is Indra's net of stars, always moving outward.
It's ourselves dead or alive who keep coming back

to re-compose the college's green grounds. A new
shape takes form, a new union when we meet

our friends' new faces, sit and enjoy their kind society.

Islington in Spring

(i)

a new wing to the house

A bright white-lit glass pyramid
surmounts the creamy-walled room,
its pine table, chairs (four), green

ficus — new leaves — beside an orange
abstract oil painting towards which leans
a brass rod to raise sky windows,

and a brass flamingo-tail will open
glass doors to a tiny walled front garden
with pots that send up fresh narcissus.

Ivory, rust, and green twine curlicues
in the Spanish floor tiles. And all this
rests hot and cool in the high sun's silver.

(ii)

looking into the back garden

A black cat sits
        on the brick-topped wall
above trellised vines,

evergreen, whose knife-leaves
        point downward.

Behind the wall, a tree-trunk
        gnarled and winter-bare
does not conceal a mass

of new white blossoms
        on another tree.

The cat turns slowly to
      regard the wild white cloud,
pointilliste, on slender branches.

Closed-in spring proliferates
      beneath still-shuttered windows
          opposite.

The Rain-wet Garden, Islington

after seeing an exhibit of Aztec sculpture

Lime-green tips overtop the side fence.
Pale stars shine, two or three, new
in dense green fernery. The white
cloud-tree thins. Its petals drop
on the brick and moss catwalk.
Low lemon-lime umbrella leaves

open over rain-washed stones laid in ochre
gravel in subtle patterns, invoking
Tlaloc, god of rain and Aztec
fears. Do we need him, his ferocity,
unpredictability, to hold off
unseen dangers? Now he's stone

dug from under a city artificially watered
and placed in a museum's perspex
cabinet. The jungle garden
teems over its boundaries. For this
the "goddess of filth," Tlazolteotl
carved in aplite, teeth bared

in hideous pain as the baby's head
comes out of her cervix, perpetual
birth shaped in pale green stone
faintly speckled as if with dirty
wash-water. She eats pollution,
frees soil from mistreatment,

"purifies transgressions" —
                    The rain-wet
garden is pure. Under its lushness
the peopled trains of London gently rumble
where water seeps down, and the diggers
keep thinking the digging is over.

Waking After a New York Poetry Reading

from lines of Denise Levertov

In the night, the poet's words
soaked in. It was like that,

I thought, waking up, although
unlike her, I didn't see my parents

standing in the doorway
but rather a line of clean light

under my windowblind,
the same as thirty years ago

when the boys banged out of bed
on Avenue C and headed off

to school, or not, if that day
one of them cut, couldn't take it—

Later in the bathroom
I was spraying stain remover

on a worn blue-green shirt
I'd dribbled down the front of,

to wash and hang it up—and saw
the furious seven-year-old run

to the rag bag, yank out his ugly
too-small rust-brown tee-shirt

with kelly green stripes and twenty
holes in it, and pull it on. His.

Mending an Umbrella

for the anniversary of my mother's death

A strut has broken.
    It cut a hole in the black cloth.
Impossible to mend, but
    the two bent ends can be wrapped together

with duct tape, so it flexes—
    but this is a waste of time. The old thing
should be tossed.
    Instead, it's a multi-winged bat, caught

under my arm, tucked tight
    so it won't flop as I try to reach in
and secure the little bar
    with a black thread-loop so it won't wobble.

My painter friend painted
    her mother as a white scrunched-up
bundle carried awkwardly.
    She hated to lay that bundle down

and feel relieved.
    It wasn't relief, exactly, to have to give
her up. The end wasn't just
    failure of a mechanism—although what else?

Because the one place
    got mended doesn't mean it offers much,
this black umbrella. Rain
    usually brings high winds, and you see them

everywhere, busted
    upside down in curbside trash baskets.
This one stands neatly
    by the hall door, an inverted exclamation-point.

Memoranda: 15 September 2001

Lower Manhattan, New York City

Four days after, near the hollow between
standing buildings—but near enough, or
too near—the pale ash lies on cars, awnings,
architraves, hubcaps, on the high lamps' long
aluminum arms, in sidewalk crevices,
on curbstones, gutters, grills, ledges under
the plateglass windows of investment banks,
on manholes, drains, fire hydrants, in cracks on
macadam beside marble steps that lead up to
the modern sculpture whose bronze geometry
blurs in dust; in every wire twist of fence
round wild weeds in a vacant lot, each grass
spike coated with fake gray snow, and bits of
flying paper, larger flakes, blow around—
Millenium Hotel, the rates for luxury
suites impaled on auto antennae, flattened
on walls, stuck in street mud, while everywhere
the nearly invisible mist of ash keeps falling
onto eyelids, eyebrows, hair, skull, and enters
stinging eyes and nostrils, ears and mouths.
The utterly pulverized, pure, fine atoms of bodies
of the dead sit on the opened tongues of the living

Takeoff, Taking In

a flight from Madeira to Paris,
soon before the birth of Ellen Ann Morley,
29 January 2003

(i)

Seated on blue-gray plastic
with pale gray plastic tray
snapped in place as the plane

shakes awake, moving along
the runway, passengers hear
three languages of safety, see

Exit, *saída, sortie,* red arrows and
video of yellow oxygen masks
and wonder when the yellow life-vest

will come into use, for safety
can't come from voices reasoning
but from the omnipotent engines,

the push, roar, the drag back against
seatbelts as the black windows pass
studded with amber lights. Liftoff

speeds power as no effort at all
for the tidy unmoving enclosure:
votre sécurité in cocoon. It goes

without seeming to go to those who
believe in help from hidden cameras'
slit eyes, *défense de fumer,* red Xs.

(ii)

Conscious of enclosure
under the reading-light,
consciousness itself breeds
the way the blood-rush circles
through the amnion, nourishes
the baby to come—the *souffle*
of waves, of airconditioning—
audible through the stethoscope
held to the pregnant mother's belly.
And here as takeoff presses
the body, the mind gestates
and develops new being, differing
fully though out of the same matrix.
The heart beats, the small fists
press, the umbilicus feeds. The time
approaches and the hoped-for safe
passage through the tight channel
and the mother's pain into the dangers
of landing—bump—in dangerous
light and air over hard fecund soil,
the exercise ground.

History

remembering the friend killed July 10, 2002
in the Sangré de Cristo mountains—
not only for his wife in mourning

A span of time. The literal
and the rupture.

(i)

fragmented mind   "heart broken"
            but
     it beats, or, that is, a muscle
            contracts
                 relaxes—

But that mountain man slipped,
  fell, struck his head, died instantly

nor does anyone know
when "it tolls for thee"—

The mountains stand, called "Blood of Christ"
     (shed, it is said, for—)

But they are far, misty and blue
  witness as one looks up
           from the cemetery gate, Rosita, Colorado
           with its sign: 1870.

Dust of pioneers mingles in mind
        at the
great cemetery where in Manahatta, 9/11/01
   the towers stood flaming
        tipped slowly, fell, thousands dead

—dead   dead—

Repeatedly the man falls
a hundred stories
         on his black-jacket wings

Video/audio tape records
    sound of the body hitting the
        ground—THUD—another, then another

Dead, dead—

and the tapes now in storage.

    What use to sit by
    the mountain man's body,
That *no-longer-he* who should not
    —she has to say it over—should not,
      like all the other young should not

  have died.

(ii)

MISSING
a xerox photo pasted on the supermarket window:

Rosalie Paisano,
    30 weeks pregnant
      [a digital banner in mind
        above Times Square, its
moving white lights, dot
    a f t e r d o t a b o v e d o t 3 0
    3 0 3 0 weeks

The dark smoke closed in—
    (You cannot save your child)
      " I cannot save—
        I   will   try ... "

No "I" now, but that
name, body, heart forever
in the ash of the gray body
no body
the weeping ghost of ash
that walks out of the smoke.

A movie reel unrolls, replays
and walks

(iii)

"…nothing to do," a woman finally, months later,
told her girl-friend, "but walk
back to Harlem

(refugee, as from
Tibet, or across Poland)
But at 57th street I began
to cramp and bleed,
and so I lost it—"

(iv)

The great gap,
the great invisible mountain of blood,
fire, flesh that
towers in the empty sky over the river

The vast sky
over the Sangré de Cristos
into which the wind
carries the mountain man's ashes

not to rise again

(v)

Stand in line. Walk out on the temporary
plywood deck. Take out a camera.
Click.
A child starts to write his name
DANIEL G

in the history
of the living who filed past
the plywood wall   but
hasn't time to finish.   The crowd has to
move on.

Develop the film.
Not a good shot. You couldn't see
to the bottom of what will never
be
buried again.

JANE AUGUSTINE is a poet and scholar whose most recent books of poetry are *Arbor Vitae* (Marsh Hawk Press, 2002) and *Transitory* (Spuyten Duyvil, 2002). Twice a winner of Fellowships in Poetry from the New York State Council on the Arts, she has also published numerous essays on H.D., Lorine Niedecker and other modern women writers. She is the editor of *The Gift by H.D.: The Complete Text* (UP Florida, 1998) and has held the H.D. Fellowship in American Literature at Beinecke Library, Yale. She lives in New York City and Westcliffe, Colorado.